It was Father Thomas Berry who suggested that we should put aside some less important things and learn to read the Earth. We agree.

The Earth's story is an extraordinary one— filled with colors that delight, music that soothes, scents that please, and breezes that excite. Our favorite characters in this story are the wild things, the things that haven't been civilized, that live and thrive without any help from us.

Wildness has something special to teach us. We have enjoyed trying to learn its lessons. We think that you will, too.

Dedicated to the people who believe in children—in their love and stirring sense of wonder.

Reading the Earth

A Story of Wildness

David R. Brower and Aleks Petrovitch

Berkeley Hills Books
Berkeley, California

The authors thank:

Darren Akana
Anne Brower
Jordy Coleman
Richard Cook
Genia and Zoe Gilbert
Jack Howell
Tsugumi Iwasaki
Gail MacKenzie
Walter Mayes

The Mill and Short Gallery
Lara Olsha
Helen Petrovitch
Maureen Regan
Herb Roth
Bill Sanchez
Willis and Lori Snyder
John Strohmeier

A portion of the royalties from the sale of this book are donated to the Earth Island Institute.

Published by

Berkeley Hills Books
P.O. Box 9877
Berkeley, California 94709
www.berkeleyhills.com

10 9 8 7 6 5 4 3 2 1

Library of Congress Catalog Card Number: 00-132044
Set in Buccaneer and Palatino
Printed in Hong Kong

Designed by Tim Ott
www.ott.to

Someone is coming.

Hey,
hello
David!

Oh good, it's Emily, George and Paolo!

Old friend, could you
please tell us one of
your stories?

Sure. Let me think of one I haven't told you. Hmmm. I've told you about my friend, Mr. Raccoon, whose leg was broken when his tree house was cut down...

And I've told you about the passenger pigeons and the magnificent California condors...

*A*h, here's a story you'll like! Why don't we pretend it took just six days to make the world we know today.

I'll tell you the Earth's story so far, take a closer look at some exciting parts, and tell you when we became part of the story ourselves.

Let's call it...

..."Reading the Earth."

Here we go! It's midnight on Sunday and suddenly the Earth begins.

How does it begin? Why?

Well, there are many wonderful explanations. All I can tell you is that it happened.

Now it's Monday. The Earth is a place of scorching heat. Then water appears. It rains for thousands of years without stopping and some amazing things happen.

Water is clever. It can come as rain and fall into lakes and streams that flow to the ocean. It can be carried as an invisible vapor from the oceans to the sky where it turns into clouds. From the clouds it can fall again as rain and snow to wash and nourish the planet.

Tuesday

On Tuesday afternoon life begins. How does this happen? I can't tell you for sure, but somehow the stuff of the Earth and the warmth of the sun come together and life is born. Tiny living cells begin to divide, multiply, add and subtract. The earth has taught them to be good at arithmetic. And all that wildness knows just what to do.

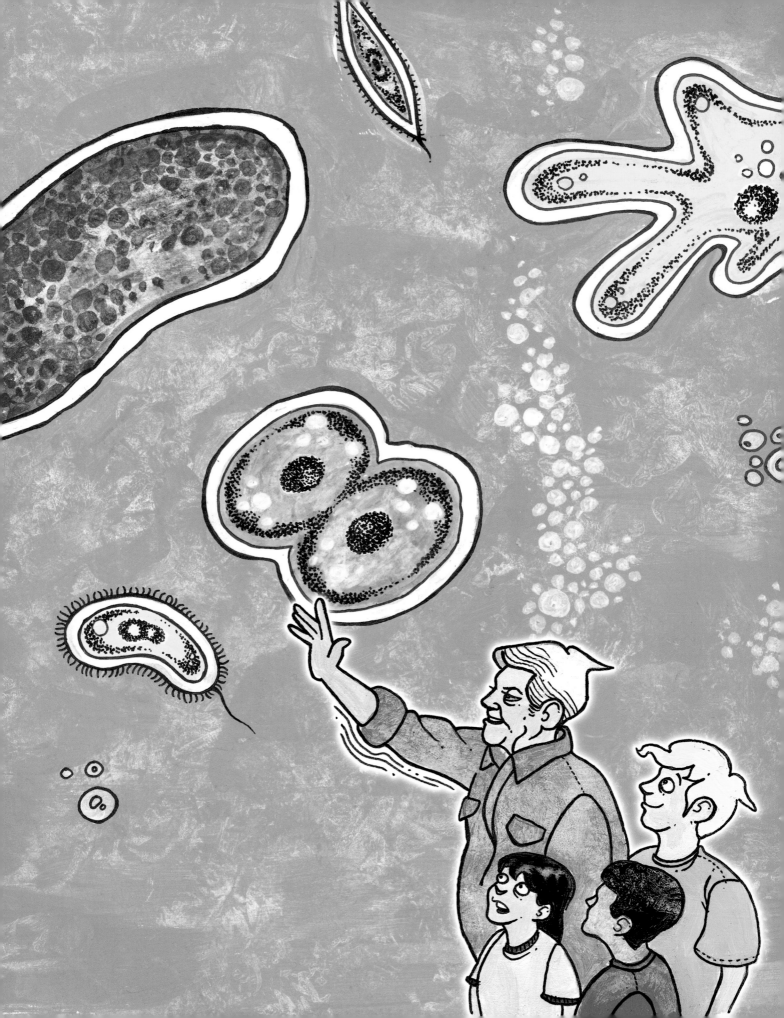

Wednesday, Thursday, Friday

On the third, fourth and fifth days, millions and millions of animals, plants and insects come to life. Some continue for many generations. Others are not so fortunate and perish as quickly as they came.

Now it's Saturday. Just imagine! Already the sixth day has started, and still many of the most amazing animals will not appear until late in the afternoon.

Here come the dinosaurs!

The dinosaurs lived for a long time on the Earth–until nine-thirty at night. These mighty animals might still be here with us if a huge asteroid hadn't crashed into the Earth from outer space.

Now it's eighteen minutes before midnight. The Grand Canyon begins to form.

Late-Late Saturday Night

We human beings appear on Earth only thirty seconds before midnight.

Even Later Saturday Night

In the last three seconds of our story so many things happen so rapidly. Humans learn to farm. Then comes the industrial revolution. Big factories pollute the air. We learn to take oil from deep in the ground and to build automobiles. We cut down forests and cover the land with pavement. We spill our wastes into the rivers and pile up trash in landfills.

Suddenly our planet is in danger.

Think of it—all these things have happened in the time it takes to count 1...2...3.

What's going to happen next?

Do you know why a living
planet is so rare?

Because of life!

How does a seed...

...know how to grow...

...into a beautiful tree?

Even though life is so complicated, it works! Think of the cells inside you that make your blood red. They know how to travel from your heart to your lungs. How to pick up oxygen, and how to deliver it wherever your body needs it.

So the tiny seed from which you grew taught your blood cells how to flow, your eyes how to see, your ears how to hear. It even keeps your tongue from being bitten while you chew.

It showed you how to become you instead of a squirrel, or a gigantic redwood tree, or any other precious form of life.

This magic web of life is the gift of the Earth. We are all part of this web, related to every other living thing. Remember those tiny cells that began on Tuesday afternoon? That was our beginning, three and a half billion years ago. Do you feel that old?

So much has come and gone. Isn't it incredible that we are still here?

Take a big
stretch.

Doesn't it feel good?

The amazing design of life was not created with formulas in a factory.

If we read the Earth we can see...

*N*ow it's midnight of the sixth day. Is the story over? No! Your story is just beginning.

Now you're in charge. What happens next is up to you. So do the best you can to preserve the wildness of the Earth for all living things and for everyone who is yet to come.

Emily, George and Paolo, what do you think of that story?

That's the most amazing story you have ever told us.

It's a lot heavier than the raccoon story.

Good-bye children. Much love!

Thanks David. Good-bye.

Hey, let's go down to the dunes.

Look at all the wildness!

Wow!

"Suddenly the Earth begins"

Men and women have always wondered how and why the Earth began. Old Chinese tradition teaches that the world came from an enormous cosmic egg. The eyes of the god Phan Ku, who was born from the egg, became the Sun and the Moon and his flesh became the Earth. The Aztecs of ancient Mexico believed in a goddess, Coatlicue, who was pulled down from the heavens and torn in half to form the Earth and sky. In India, it is said that a god named Prajapati was born from a golden egg and, by speaking his first word, made the Earth. Jews and Christians teach that God created the world in six days.

According to scientists, the Earth began about four and a half billion years ago when gases, dust and other particles circling the Sun became packed together to form the sphere we call home. David follows this timeline in *Reading the Earth*, dividing it into six days. Each day in his story is 750 million years long.

"The new Earth is a place of scorching heat"

For almost a billion years the Earth was too hot for any living thing to survive on it. Meteorites flying through outer space collided with the boiling planet and volcanoes exploded across its landscape. There was no air to breathe, nothing to drink, and the sun's rays burned hot across its surface. Before life might find a home here, the world needed to cool, and its climate needed to stabilize so that plants and animals might grow and reproduce safely.

"Then water appears"

As the Earth cooled, volcanic activity across the land calmed. Water formed pools, streams, lakes and seas. Steamy water turned to clouds and rain fell. Clouds and other gases formed the atmosphere, which blanketed the Earth, protecting it from the Sun's harshest rays. Protected and nourished by water, the planet was ready to welcome the arrival of life and all its creatures.

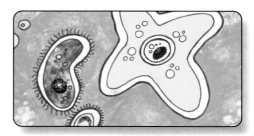

"On Tuesday afternoon life begins"

The origins of life have been explained in many ways. Many traditions ascribe it to the workings of powerful gods or goddesses. The discoveries of scientists suggest that life first appeared on Earth about three and a half billion years ago. The oldest forms of life were simple kinds of bacteria, tiny organisms too small to see. They lived in shallow water, and produced their food by absorbing sunlight and combining it with elements that surrounded them. From these microscopic creatures, over billions of years, the wonderful variety of living things we see today evolved — every rose, every maple tree, every salmon, every bear and every giraffe.

The presence of life makes the Earth different from every other place in the universe that has yet been discovered. Scientists believe, however, that as we explore further into space and its many billions of planets, we are likely to find other places where life exists.

"Here come the dinosaurs"

Dinosaurs walked the Earth for about 160 million years. Some were meat-eaters, but the largest of all lived by eating plants. The longest, the diplodocus, was nearly 100 feet from nose to tail. The biggest, the brachiosaurus, weighed 88 tons, as large as seventeen elephants. Among flying dinosaurs, the Big Bend pterosaur was the size of a small airplane — almost forty feet from one wing tip to the other. Why the dinosaurs died out 65 million years ago is a great mystery. It may have been a result of changing sea level or climate, or of the arrival of new and dangerous predators. One current theory holds that a large asteroid or comet from space may have struck the Earth, bringing an end to the dinosaurs and disrupting living systems around the world.

"The Grand Canyon begins to form"

The Grand Canyon in northern Arizona is the largest canyon in the world. It is 277 miles long, one mile deep, and as much as eighteen miles wide. Created by the flow of the Colorado River and the rising up of the plateau through which it cuts, this dramatic natural wonder was formed in less than six million years.

Traditional home to the Havasupai people, the Grand Canyon was found by Spanish explorers in 1540. In 1869, geologist John Wesley Powell and his crew traveled the length of the canyon in four boats, completing a journey over raging, white waters that had previously been thought impossible.

In recent years, the construction of Glen Canyon Dam, further up the Colorado River, has threatened the natural life of the Grand Canyon. Because of this dam, and heavy tourist use, the Grand Canyon will require great care to preserve for future generations.

"We human beings appear"

The origins of humanity have been explained in many ways by different people at different times. The ancient Greeks said that men and women were created by the god Prometheus, who separated us from the rest of the animals by giving us fire. The Native Americans of the southwestern U.S. taught that the first men and women on Earth came from the underworld, in search of a new beginning after creating difficulties in their subterranean life. The Hebrew tradition is that God breathed life upon dust to create the first man.

Among contemporary scientists there are several theories about the origins of mankind. Cases have been made for the first humans appearing in Southern Africa, southeastern Asia, and the Middle East, and from these points spreading to other parts of the Earth. There is strong evidence that the first *homo sapiens* appeared about 200,000 years ago.

"Then comes the industrial revolution"

The eighteenth century brought one of the most important events in human history — the industrial revolution. Before then, the world's economy was based on small farms, hand-powered craftsmanship and regional trade. With the discovery of the principles of steam- and coal-powered machinery, and the mastery of ironmaking, humanity began to shift from rural areas to cities, from handmade to machine-made goods, and from working in small shops and farms to working in large factories.

This change, which has brought many benefits, has also given us large industrial plants and ways of living that consume enormous amounts of the Earth's limited natural resources. We also release into the air, rivers and soil great quantities of polluting waste. Before the industrial revolution and the introduction of huge manufacturing enterprises, the health of the Earth was not at risk.

"Suddenly our planet is in danger"

Because of human actions the well-being of the Earth is threatened as never before. Our use of oil and coal to generate power and fuel our automobiles has caused a rise in global temperature that may cause problems in the health of many plants and animals, as well as ourselves. The cutting down of forests and the conversion of farms into housing and business developments also tempt us with short-term rewards at the expense of long-term environmental safety.

As more land is paved, more energy and resources are consumed, and more factories are built without environmental safeguards (often in other parts of the world), we come closer to destroying those gifts of the Earth that make life possible and cannot be replaced.

"How does a seed know how to grow"

Although seeds are among the most common things that surround us, they are miracles of nature. About 235,000 different plants bear seeds. Within each seed are the beginnings of each part of the plant — the root, stems and leaves-and a food supply that supports the young plant until it can live on its own. Seeds are also covered with hard shells to protect them until they are ready to open. Many plants do not produce seeds — ferns and mosses, for example — but because seeds are so efficient, plants that use them are dominant in the natural world.

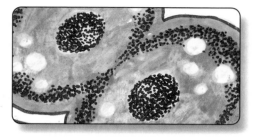

"Think of the cells inside you"

Every person, and every living plant and animal, is made up of cells. Cells are tiny factories that singly or in large groups carry on all the processes necessary for life. Cells in our body digest our food, process our waste, control our breathing and nourish our muscles. As the cells that make up our bodies divide and reproduce, we grow. Although most cells are far too small to see, some are large indeed. An egg, for example, is a cell out of which can grow a fully-formed animal.

"What happens next is up to you"

In your life, you will be faced with many choices that have an impact on the health of the Earth. It will be up to you and the people you know to preserve parks and farmlands, to limit the amount of pollution that is released into rivers and the air, and to halt the destruction of forests and animal species upon which the balance of life on Earth depends.

The more you know the more you can help. You might begin by learning to read the Earth itself — to discover its beauty and wonder, and to understand how, in its wild way, it sustains us all.

Youth environmental organizations can also help you to understand our planet and to take action in meaningful ways to protect it. Here are several such groups with their website addresses. You are likely to find others active in your community.

Check out these organizations:

- Youth for Environmental Sanity — **www.yesworld.org**
- Youth for Environmental Service — **www.yes1.org**
- The Surfrider Foundation — **www.surfrider.org**
- The Earthsavers Club of the National Wildlife Federation — **www.nwf.org/earthsavers**
- Earth Island Institute — **www.earthisland.org**
- Wildness Within — **www.wildnesswithin.com**